This book is dedicated to my
dearest friend and mother,
Earline Hill

ISBN 978-1-63625-108-0

Book design by Ryan Swint

Your Hair is Your Crown!

By Tamekia Swint

Illustrated by Ashley Bailey

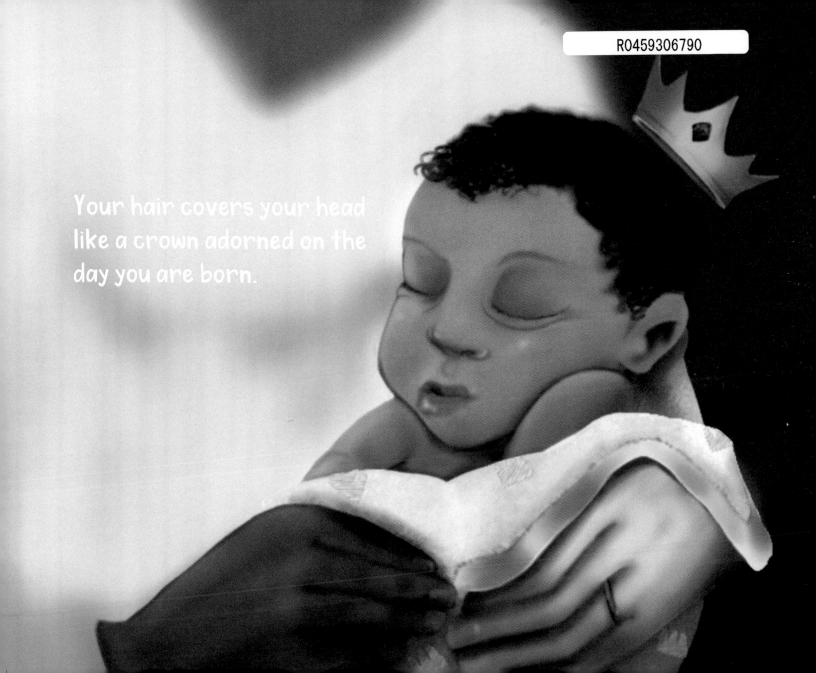

Your hair covers your head like a crown adorned on the day you are born.

You are strong, and you are turning three.

Your curls are getting longer and super coily.

Keep your head up and try not to frown. You can do it!

Your hair is your crown!

Your hair is long, but you like it cut short. Your barber enthusiastically shows his support!

Your hair is your crown!

Your bonnet protects your hair, and your durag keeps it tied down.

You protect your style because...

Your hair is your crown!

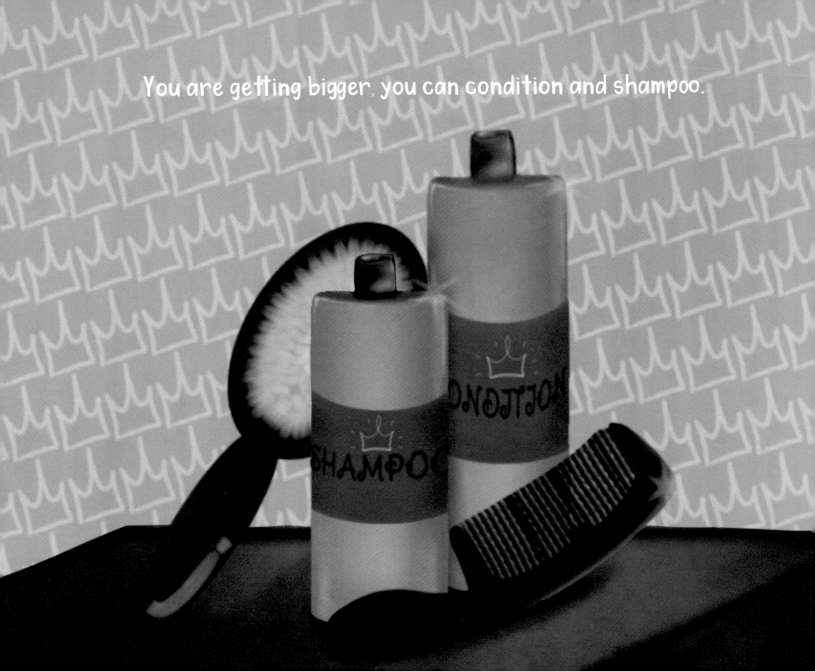

You are getting bigger, you can condition and shampoo.

You can wear your hair so many different ways!
You can wear it straight, curly, short, or in braids.
You moisturize it every day!

Your hair shows the world who you are and who you will be.

You feel grown-up, confident, and free!

You can color your hair green, red, blond, or blue.
It truly reflects a picture of you. Yes, it is true.

You are powerful, unique, and one of a kind!

You were born with a purpose, put here by design.

When you look at yourself, you will see images of your family.
Your hair is part of your heritage, your culture, and your identity.
Your skin is beautifully brown don't you see?

Your hair is your crown!

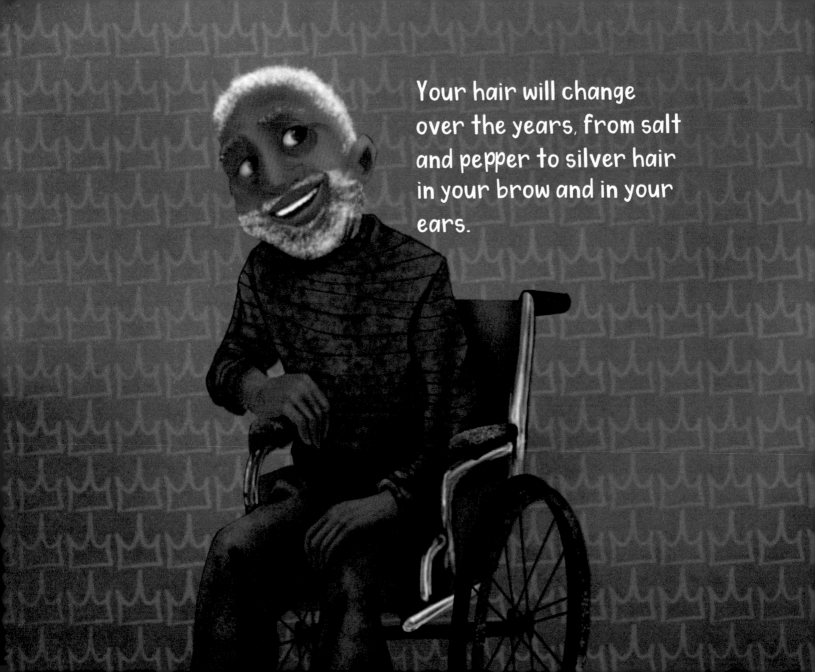

Your hair will change over the years, from salt and pepper to silver hair in your brow and in your ears.

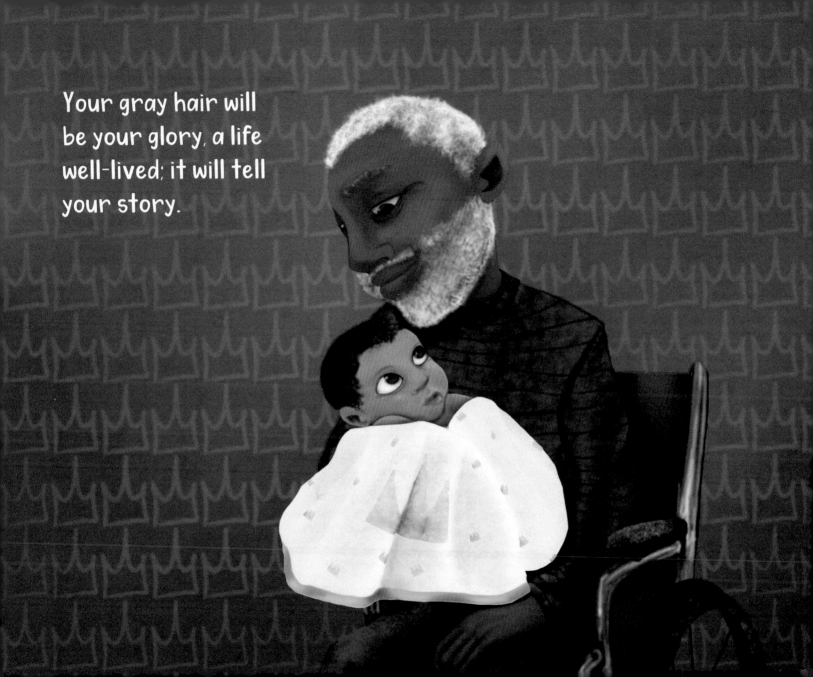

Your gray hair will be your glory, a life well-lived; it will tell your story.

Place your
picture here

Your hair is your crown!

ABOUT THE AUTHOR

Tamekia Swint is a wife, mom, hairstylist, and instructor who is passionate about hair! In 2010 Tamekia founded Styles 4 Kidz, a non-profit organization that provides textured hair care resources, services, and education for kids in the transracial adoptive, foster, and biracial community. Tamekia has loved braiding hair from a young age and is committed to helping kids grow their confidence and love how they look through beautiful hairstyles. She is a Chicago native whose love for writing and gift for hairstyling is on full display in her writing debut, "Your Hair is Your Crown!" This book is a gift to every child she has served over the last fifteen years. Tamekia will donate a portion of the profit from book sales to Styles4Kidz.

Learn more at www.styles4kidz.org.